# ANNIE AND I

## ALLOTMENT ADVENTURE WITH
# MR GREEN &
## SHELLY THE SUNFLOWER

Written by Janet Ward
Illustrated by TitanFahmi

It was early morning down
at the allotment. As the moon went to sleep and the
new day was about to begin the birds
began to sweetly sing their morning song.

As the first rays of sunshine broke through and the
gentle morning breeze whispered, the allotments began
to wake up.Spiders were busily weaving delicate, silky
webs. Butterflies fluttered and bees buzzed.

Shelly Sunflower lifted her head. She smiled at the
morning sun and the beautiful blue sky. With her soft
yellow petals and her warm friendly smile, she brought
happiness to everyone who saw her.

Shelly Sunflower gently shook her vibrant green leaves,
shaking off the sparkling drops
of morning dew. She knew that
today was going to be a good day.

Today was a special day. It was open day. A day for people to come along and look at the delights the allotments had to offer.

Mr Green worked hard growing his vegetables and flowers. Like all the other allotments, his was a remarkable sight with vegetables of every description and flowers that were a rainbow of colours.

Mr Green looked around; he was immensely proud. He glanced up at Shelly Sunflower as she danced and smiled. Mr Green stroked his beard thoughtfully; he knew that today something special was about to happen.

As he set about his work and was busy giving the runner beans a drink from his watering can he heard voices coming from the gate.

"Hello there," Mr Green called. Leaning on the gate were two small children, they did not look happy! Their faces were frowning! Behind them stood their mum and dad.

"Good morning," replied mum. "We have brought twins, Annie, and Fin to learn about vegetables, and see where they come from and how they are grown.

"We do not like vegetables" moaned Annie! Screwing up her face. "Vegetables are all green and boring, they taste disgusting YUK!"
snapped Fin.

"What a beautiful sunflower" mum said,
staring up at Shelly.
Shelly smiled down at the twins.
She waved her leaves, welcoming them onto
the allotment. Shelly tried her best to cheer
them up, but it was no use!

The twin's minds were made up and could not
be changed. Or could they?

Mr Green opened the gate
and invited the family in to have a look around. He
explained how he planted tiny seeds and how with the
help of the sun and rain he watched as if by magic
they grew into healthy vegetables and beautiful
blooming flowers.

How Shelly Sunflower makes everyone feel happy with
her sweet smile and how he watched the bees collect
pollen to make delicious honey.
Mr Green told the twins that not all vegetables are
green and boring but how they help make us grow
strong and stay healthy.

"Can you imagine what they might say if they could
talk?" he asked.
"Really" groaned Annie. Talking vegetables, HUH!" Mr
Green looked at Shelly Sunflower.
He stroked his beard thoughtfully
and Shelly smiled.

A gentle breeze blew.
The runner beans shook themselves.
They dangled and danced as their leaves
twisted and tangled themselves around
the tall sticks that held them up.
"Pick me whispered a quiet voice. Annie and Fins eyes
opened wide. They looked around."Who said that " they
gasped."Pick me" The voice said again, a little louder.
"Please I want to be your friend."
The twins looked at Mr Green. He pointed toward the
runner beans. They reached up and took one.
"What is it " they asked.

Hello, my name is Runner Bean
There is more to me than just being green
I need a friend give me a go
Eat me I will help you grow
I am healthy I am tasty too
Pick me, taste me, try a few
I'm runner bean, I'm green,
I'm trendy Pick me I am really friendly
I'm runner bean, I'm green, I'm long, eat me,
you'll grow big and strong
Annie and Fin stared at
each other in amazement!

Mr Green the Gardener looked
at Shelly Sunflower. He stroked his beard
and Shelly smiled.
Still shocked at what had just happened Annie and Fin
followed Mr Green, he pointed towards a patch of soft, green
wispy plants that were growing out from the ground. He
gently loosened the ground with his garden fork."Pull me up
carefully" came a voice. Annie and Fin gasped.
Their faces were not frowning now, instead they were full of
wonder and smiles.
Together they carefully pulled. From out of the ground and
still clinging to the green wispy plant was something orange.
"So, vegetables are green, and boring, are they?" chuckled a
cheeky voice." Well, I am not green, and I am not boring!"

Hello, I'm carrot, I'm not a bore
Boil me, roast me, eat me raw
It 's me I'm Carrot, if you are wise
Eat me, I am good for your eyes
If you fancy a snack with a bit of a crunch
Try a few carrot sticks, to eat with your lunch, I am carrot, eat me raw
Once you have tried me You'll be wanting more.
Annie and Fin stared at each other; their eyes open wide
'We didn't know carrots grew underground,
the wispy green plant looks like its hair,'
laughed Annie."I think carrots are fun!"

Mr Green the gardener looked up
at Shelly sunflower, He stroked
his beard and Sally smiled.
"What 's next?" The children asked excitedly.
They skipped towards some green leaves with veins of deep
red running through them.
"Please Mr Green...." before they could finish their sentence Mr
Green the gardener gently loosened the soil with his garden
fork."Hey down here" called the voice "bet you can't guess
what I am?"Annie and Fin could hardly wait! They took hold of
the leaves and gave a gentle tug, from out of the ground came
something round, the children looked puzzled.

I grow in the ground My colour is Red
My shape is round
It's me, I'm beetroot
I grow in the ground...
Full of vitamin C
Packed with nutrients
I will keep you healthy
A great source of fibre, try me and see
I am good for your blood
I am beetroot that is me You have no excuse
Not to pickle me, crisp me
Or make delicious juice
"Beetroot crisps I'll give those a try!"
Fin said licking his lips.

Mr Green the gardener looked up
at Shelly Sunflower, he stroked his beard
and Shelly smiled.
"We have to be going soon" Mum told the children
"Oh but we are learning about vegetables just like you wanted, it 's
fun please let us stay a little longer!" begged the children.
"Just one more then" agreed Mum.
Annie and Fin spotted a group of tall plants. They had strange looking
things growing on them.
"Dad these plants are as tall as you" called Fin.
Dad stood amongst the plants, the leaves tickled his face. Annie and
Fin giggled.
"Take me, pull me off " whispered a voice. The children gently pulled.
"No idea what this could be?" Fin said shaking his head.

Hi I'm Sweetcorn
I'm a very nice fellow
Peel off my green leaves
Find my corn, it's bright yellow
Not sure how to eat me
I will give you some clues
You can roast me, grill me
I taste great barbecued.
Annie and Fin carefully peeled back the green
leaves to find the sweetcorn as yellow as the sun.
It was like finding gold..

Mr Green looked at Shelly Sunflower.
He stroked his beard and Shelly smiled.
"OK you two it really is time to go now". The children
looked disappointed. Suddenly a wave of scrumptious
smells swept across the allotments.

"Hmm! What is that delicious mouth-watering smell?"
mum asked. "Where is that coming from?" asked the
children as their noses twitched and their stomachs
grumbled. Mr Green pointed towards a large shed.
Annie, Fin, Mum, and Dad followed the smell, their
noses sniffing the fragrant air. Mr green strolled
closely behind. They reached the large shed where
there a banquet of colourful treats.

Mrs Clarke the cook invited the family to come and
taste the delights. Everything here is made from the
vegetables grown on Mr Greens amazing allotment of
wonders.

Sweetcorn sizzled on the barbecue, runner beans simmered in a delicious vegetable curry, beetroot crisps and beetroot juice as red as a deep red rose tempted Annie and Fin. "Mmm these crunchy beetroot crisps taste delicious so yummy you have to try them" they said licking their lips. "This vegetable curry makes your taste buds tingle; we have to make this at home" called Dad wiping his mouth clean. Mum could not answer she was too busy crunching crispy carrot sticks while Fin sipped beetroot juice trying not to spill any.

Finally, they tasted the sweetcorn that had been sizzling on the barbecue. With the taste explosions still bursting on their tongues it was time to say goodbye.

The family thanked Mrs Clarke the cook for letting them experience the taste of the allotments "we never would have known how good vegetables could taste, we are very grateful". Annie and Fin looked at Mr Green, "please can we visit your allotment again?" they asked politely. "We had no idea growing vegetables could be such fun".

"I would be happy to see you again there is still so much to show you. Still so many vegetables, plants, insects and animals for you to meet and learn about ". Mum, Dad, Annie and Fin waved goodbye "see you soon for some more allotment adventures" they shouted happily.

Back at the allotment Mr Green was feeling very proud, he looked at Shelly as she danced, waving her leaves. Mr Green the gardener stroked his beard thoughtfully and Shelly Sunflower smiled. They knew that today had been a good day.

Printed in Great Britain
by Amazon